CH00794697

Flavour

SUFF

RECIPES

Compiled by Julia Skinner

THE FRANCIS FRITH COLLECTION

www.francisfrith.com

First published in the United Kingdom in 2012 by The Francis Frith Collection®

This edition published exclusively for Identity Books in 2012 ISBN 978-1-84589-679-9

Text and Design copyright The Francis Frith Collection®
Photographs copyright The Francis Frith Collection® except where indicated.

The Frith® photographs and the Frith® logo are reproduced under licence from
Heritage Photographic Resources Ltd, the owners of the Frith® archive and trademarks.
'The Francis Frith Collection', 'Francis Frith' and 'Frith' are registered trademarks of
Heritage Photographic Resources Ltd.

All rights reserved. No photograph in this publication may be sold to a third party other than in the original
form of this publication, or framed for sale to a third party. No parts of this publication may be reproduced,
stored in a retrieval system, or transmitted, in any form, or by any means, electronic, mechanical, photocopying,
recording or otherwise, without the prior permission of the publishers and copyright holder.

British Library Cataloguing in Publication Data

Flavours of Suffolk - Recipes
Compiled by Julia Skinner

The Francis Frith Collection
Oakley Business Park
Wylye Road, Dinton,
Wiltshire SP3 5EU
Tel: +44 (0) 1722 716 376
Email: info@francisfrith.co.uk
www.francisfrith.com

Printed and bound in Malaysia
Contains material sourced from responsibly managed forests

Front Cover: **LEISTON, SIZEWELL ROAD 1922** 72579p
Frontispiece: **IPSWICH, THE ANCIENT HOUSE 1921** 70398
Contents: **FLATFORD, THE MILL 1907** 57551

The colour-tinting is for illustrative purposes only, and is not intended to be historically accurate

AS WITH ANY HISTORICAL DATABASE, THE FRANCIS FRITH ARCHIVE IS CONSTANTLY BEING
CORRECTED AND IMPROVED, AND THE PUBLISHERS WOULD WELCOME INFORMATION ON
OMISSIONS OR INACCURACIES

CONTENTS

RECIPE

PARSNIP AND APPLE SOUP

Suffolk is a region of fertile farmland with much arable land under cultivation. Wheat, barley, oil-seed rape and sugar beet are particularly important crops, as well as a wide range of vegetables. Root crops such as potatoes, parsnips and carrots are widely grown, as well as salad crop and brassicas. This recipe combines the flavour of parsnips with the slight tartness of a cooking apple to make a tasty soup for cold winter days. You can also spice it up with a little curry powder if you like, stirred into the pan with the vegetables and cooked for a minute or so before the stock is added.

675g/1½ lbs parsnips, trimmed, peeled and roughly chopped
25g/1oz butter
1 large cooking apple, cored, peeled and roughly chopped
1.2 litres/2 pints chicken or vegetable stock
4 fresh sage leaves, left whole, or half a teaspoonful dried sage
150ml/5 fl oz/ ¼ pint single cream
Salt and pepper
1 tablespoonful finely chopped fresh parsley, to garnish

Melt the butter in a large saucepan, add the chopped parsnips and apple, cover the pan with its lid and cook over a gentle heat for 10 minutes, stirring occasionally to prevent sticking. Add the stock and sage (leaving the leaves whole, if using fresh sage). Bring to the boil, cover reduce the heat and simmer for about 30 minutes, until the parsnip is well softened. Remove the sage leaves and leave the soup to cool down a bit, then process it through a blender or liquidizer until it is smooth. Return the soup to the pan, stir in the cream and season to taste. Reheat before serving but do not allow the soup to boil. Serve the soup hot, garnished with finely chopped fresh parsley

WALBERSWICK, THE FRUIT AND VEG STALL 1919 69128x

RECIPE

SPINACH SOUP WITH DUMPLINGS

This tasty soup from Suffolk is traditionally served with small dumplings that are cooked in it just before dishing up. You might like to follow the example of country people in the past by adding a few handfuls of nettle tops to the soup as well, if you are making it in the spring – the shoots of young nettles have been cooked and eaten in the early spring by country people for centuries as a welcome and nutritious source of fresh greens during the 'hungry gap', the time of year before other vegetables are ready to eat. Only the tender top sprigs should be picked (wearing gloves!) and eaten, and can be cooked in the same way as spinach, or made into a tasty soup, as given here. And don't worry about eating them – the acid which causes the nettles to sting is destroyed by cooking. Serves 4.

> 450g/1 lb spinach (plus a few nettle tops, if using)
> 1 onion, peeled and finely chopped
> 1 carrot, trimmed and chopped into small pieces
> 1 stick of celery, trimmed and chopped into small pieces
> 1 dessertspoonful finely chopped fresh parsley
> Half a teaspoonful finely chopped thyme
> 25g/1oz uncooked long grain rice
> 900ml/1½ pints chicken or vegetable stock
> 25g/1oz butter
> Salt and pepper

Wash the spinach (and nettle tops, if using), remove any tough ribs and stalks, and roughly chop it. Put the vegetables in a large pan with the herbs, rice and stock. Bring to the boil, stirring, then cover the pan, reduce the heat and simmer for 30 minutes, stirring regularly. Take the pan off the heat and allow the soup to cool a little, then process it through a blender or liquidizer until smooth. Return the soup to the pan, stir in the butter and season to taste. Now make the dumplings. (If you don't want to bother with the dumplings, reheat the soup now and serve.)

For the dumplings:
115g/4oz self raising flour
50g/2oz shredded suet
A pinch of salt
A little water, to mix

To make the dumplings, mix the flour, salt and suet with just enough cold water to form a firm dough. Flour your hands and shape the dough into 8 small balls, and roll them in a little extra flour. Bring the soup to the boil and drop in the dumplings. Cover the pan, reduce the heat to simmer and cook the dumplings in the soup for 15-20 minutes. Test by sticking one with a fork – if it comes out clean, the dumplings are cooked. Serve the soup, adding two dumplings with each portion.

WOODBRIDGE, THE CROSS INN, CHURCH STREET 1906 53497x

**LOWESTOFT
LONDON ROAD NORTH
1896** 37924

MARINA HOUSE.
Mrs F. PEACOCK.
FANCY DRAPER.
MILLINER.
DRESSMAKER.
Ladies & Childrens
OUTFITTER.

THE MARINA

Mrs PEACOCK
FANCY DRAPER

& LADIE

RECIPE

HERRINGS WITH MUSTARD SAUCE

Suffolk had a thriving fishing industry in the past, and the herring trade in particular made the fortunes of several coastal towns, especially Lowestoft. By the 1880s Lowestoft was estimated to have had 312 drifters and 139 trawlers. After a fishing trip, the drifters unloaded their haul into specially made wicker baskets for herrings known as 'swills', which were unique to Lowestoft and its close Norfolk neighbour, Great Yarmouth. The herring season lasted from September to November, during which every available space in the town was used to process the herring. Gutting, pickling and packing were done by women – mainly Scots – who followed the herring boats down the coast. This was a skilled job, and a good herring woman could gut 40 fish a minute. The women bandaged their hands to protect them against the brine, and as they were on piece-rate it was essential to keep their fingers nimble. This they did by continuously knitting in their free time. A favourite way of cooking Lowestoft herrings in the past was to boil them in sea water, which kept their flesh firm, and then serve them with a tangy mustard sauce, a traditional accompaniment to herrings in many parts of England. Serves 4.

4 large herrings
1.2 litres/2 pints of water
115g/4oz salt

For the mustard sauce
25g/1oz butter
25g/1oz plain flour
300ml/ ½ pint milk
  (or fish stock, if preferred)
1 heaped teaspoonful dry
  mustard powder
1 dessertspoonful white wine
  vinegar
1 teaspoonful caster sugar
1 teaspoonful lemon juice
3 tablespoonfuls double cream
  (optional)
Salt and pepper

Remove the heads, tails and fins from the cleaned fish, split them open along the belly, from head to tail, and remove the guts. Spread the fish out on a board, cut side down, and press with your fingers down the backbone. Turn the fish over and remove the backbone by easing it up with your fingers. Most of the small bones will also come away as well. Put the water and salt into a large pan and bring to the boil. Put in the herrings, bring the water back to the boil and cook the fish at a fast boil for 10 minutes. If there is not enough water to cover the fish, add more boiling water and a little more salt.

Whilst the fish are cooking, make the mustard sauce. Melt the butter in a saucepan. Stir in the flour, and gradually add the milk (or fish stock), a little at a time, stirring continuously. Bring to the boil, stirring, until the sauce thickens, then simmer for 2 minutes. Remove from heat. Blend the mustard powder, sugar, vinegar and lemon juice to a smooth cream and mix well into the sauce. Stir in the cream just before serving, if using. Season the sauce to taste and heat through before serving, but do not let the sauce boil.

When the fish are cooked, drain them well and serve hot, with the mustard sauce poured over them.

LOWESTOFT, DRIFTERS c1955 L105112

RECIPES

SOUSED HERRINGS

This was a popular way of preparing fresh herrings in East Anglia in the past, allowing a glut of herrings to be cooked and preserved. It makes an ideal lunch or supper dish, and once the herrings have been 'soused', they can be kept in the fridge for several days if necessary. Lowestoft used to be famous for its mackerel industry as well as for herrings, and fresh mackerel can also be prepared the same way.

> 4 herrings (or mackerel), filleted
> 25g/1oz plain flour
> Half a teaspoonful of powdered mace
> 25g/1oz butter
> Salt and pepper
> 1 teaspoonful of chopped fresh parsley
> 1 bay leaf
> 150ml/ ¼ pint water
> 150ml/ ¼ pint malt vinegar

Pre-heat the oven to 190°C/375°F/Gas Mark 5.

Mix the flour with the salt, pepper and mace, and use it to dust the herring fillets. Place a small knob of butter in the centre of each fillet, sprinkle the fillet with chopped parsley and roll it up, skin side out. Secure each herring roll with a wooden cocktail stick. Place the herrings in an ovenproof dish, and add the water, vinegar and bay leaf. Cover the dish and bake for 1 hour in the pre-heated oven. Remove from the oven and leave the herrings to cool completely in the cooking liquid before serving. Eat cold, serve with slices of bread and butter.

KIPPER SAVOURY

Another way of preserving herrings is to smoke them and turn them into kippers, and curing or smoking herring began at an early stage in Lowestoft's development. The process involved fish being hung over the smoke from slowly burning oak and ash wood. The fires would burn for up to a month with the occasional dowsing to remove the fat dripping from the fish.

> 2 large kippers
> 50g/2oz butter
> 1 tablespoonful of chopped chives
> Half a clove of garlic, crushed with a few grains of salt
> 225g/8oz plain flour
> 75g/3oz lard or margarine
> 75g/3oz peeled and grated raw potato
> About 1 tablespoonful cold water
> A little melted butter to finish

Pre-heat the oven to 200°C/400°F/Gas Mark 6.

Simmer the kipper fillets in boiling water until the flesh comes away from the bones easily; alternatively, steam the kippers between two plates over a pan of simmering water for about 20 minutes. Remove flesh, and discard the bones and skin. Soften the butter gently in a basin, but do not let it melt to oil. Add the flaked kipper flesh, the chopped chives and crushed garlic, and mix well. Rub the lard or margarine into the flour, add the grated potato and mix it all to a firm dough with a little water. Roll out half the dough and line a pie plate about 20-22cms (7-8 inches) in diameter. Spread the filling onto the pastry, not quite to the edge, and dampen the edge of the pastry with cold water. Roll out the remaining dough and use it to make a cover, press the edges together to seal well, and trim and flute the edge. Using the tip of a sharp knife, make a criss-cross pattern on top of the pie cutting through the lid to the filling, to resemble a fishing net. Brush the top of the pastry with a little melted butter, and bake in the pre-heated oven for about 35 minutes, until the pastry is crisp and golden. This is good served with parsley sauce.

RECIPE

FISHERMAN'S PIE

A wide variety of fish is caught by Suffolk fishermen, although the county's fishing fleet is a fraction of what it was in the past. Catches might include sole, skate, bass, plaice, whiting, haddock and cod in season. You can buy locally landed fresh fish and shellfish at several places along the Suffolk coast, such as Lowestoft, Orford, Southwold and Aldeburgh, which is particularly famous for its fresh cod, especially in the winter. This fish pie was traditionally made with cod or haddock, or a mixture of both, but these fish are now in short supply and thus expensive. If you prefer, use a cheaper and more sustainable white fish, such as whiting, coley or pollock.

For the filling:
675g/1½ lbs cod or haddock fillets, or alternative white fish (see above)
600ml/1 pint milk
1 bay leaf
Half an onion, finely sliced
3 hard-boiled eggs, chopped
75g/3oz butter or margarine
50g/2oz plain flour
1 level tablespoonful capers, drained and chopped
3 tablespoonfuls finely chopped fresh parsley
1 dessertspoonful lemon juice

For the topping:
675g/1½ lbs potatoes, freshly boiled until tender
50g/2oz butter
60ml/ 4 tablespoonfuls milk
Salt and pepper

Pre-heat the oven to 180°C/350°F/Gas Mark 4.

Place the milk, the bay leaf and sliced onion in a large saucepan over a medium heat, season with salt and pepper and add the fish. Cover, and poach the fish lightly for 10 minutes. Strain, discard the bay leaf and onion pieces and reserve the milk for the sauce. Flake the fish into fairly large pieces into a large, deep buttered pie dish, discarding the skin and any remaining bones. Cover the fish with the slices of hard boiled egg.

ALDEBURGH, THE BEACH 1906 56817

Melt 75g/3oz butter in a saucepan on a low heat, stir in the flour and cook gently for 1 minute, stirring continually. Remove the pan from the heat and stir in the reserved milk the fish was poached in, a little at a time and stirring continually so no lumps are formed. When all the milk is mixed in, return the pan to the heat and bring the mixture to the boil, stirring continually as the sauce thickens, then simmer the sauce for about 4 minutes, still stirring all the time. Remove from the heat and stir in the chopped capers, parsley, lemon juice and seasoning to taste. Pour the sauce over the fish and eggs in the pie dish so that it is evenly covered. Make the topping by mashing the cooked potatoes with the butter and milk, and beat until smooth. Spoon the mashed potato over the fish mixture to cover, then score the surface with a fork to rough it up. Bake the pie on a high shelf in the pre-heated oven for 25-30 minutes, until the top is crisp and golden.

RECIPE

CRISPY FRIED SPRATS

Sprats are caught all along the East Anglian coast, but Aldeburgh and Southwold are particularly famous for these small fish, a cousin of the herring. The first sprats of the season used to be sent from Aldeburgh to London for the Lord Mayor's Banquet on 9th November every year, which was known irreverently by Londoners as 'Sprat Day'. Sprats are cheap and in season between October and March. They are very good coated in seasoned flour or oatmeal and then fried until crisp, sprinkled with lemon juice and eaten for tea or supper with slices of brown bread and butter.

> 450g/1lb sprats
> 25g/1oz plain flour or fine oatmeal
> Salt and pepper
> Oil for deep frying
> Lemon wedges

Wash the sprats well, then cut off their heads and remove the guts at the same time. This is called 'drawing' them, and is done by cutting through the top of the body, just behind the head, but not quite cutting through the belly. The knife is then used to pull the head away from the body and the inside will be drawn out at the same time. After a bit of practice it just takes a few seconds to deal with each fish. Now pat the fish dry with kitchen paper. Season the flour or oatmeal with salt and pepper, and toss the sprats in it, a few at a time, until each fish is coated. Heat 2cms (½ inch) of oil in a large frying pan until it is just smoking. Add a small batch of fish and fry for 2-3 minutes, until they are crisp and golden brown on both sides. Lift them out with a fish slice, drain well and keep them hot in a dish lined with kitchen paper whilst you fry the rest of the sprats in batches, draining them well before transferring them to your serving dish to keep hot. Sprinkle the cooked sprats with salt to keep them crisp, and serve with lemon wedges and slices of brown bread and butter.

RECICE

SUFFOLK PERCH

This is an old Suffolk recipe for perch, widely considered to be the best of freshwater fish after salmon and trout. Perch are seldom available from fishmongers, but they are delicious fish with a tasty white meat, due to the fresh, clear water in which they live. If you know an angler who can catch you some, try this way of cooking perch in cyder, as it is spelled in Suffolk. Cyder made in Suffolk, such as that made by the award-winning Aspall Cyder Company near Stowmarket, uses juice from cooking or dessert apple varieties and so has a less astringent character than the cider made elsewhere in England, which uses juice from sharp cider apples. Serves 4.

> 4 perch, each about 225g/8oz in weight
> 2 tablespoonfuls cooking oil
> 4 tomatoes, skinned and chopped
> 2 medium onions, peeled and chopped
> A sprig of fresh thyme
> Salt and pepper
> 115g/4oz soft herring roes
> 50g/2oz fresh brown breadcrumbs
> 450ml/ ¾ pint Suffolk cyder
> 1 dessertspoonful finely chopped fresh parsley, to garnish

Pre-heat the oven to 180°C/350°F/Gas Mark 4.

As the perch is difficult to scale, plunge the fish into boiling water for a few minutes to loosen the scales. Clean and gut the fish. Heat the oil in a flameproof casserole dish and add the tomatoes, onions, sprig of thyme, salt and pepper. Simmer over a low heat for 15 minutes. Mix the soft herring roes and breadcrumbs in a bowl. Add 1 tablespoonful of the tomato and onion mixture from the dish, mix well and season. Stuff the cavities of the fish with the mixture. Lay the fish on top of the remaining tomato and onion mixture in the casserole dish and pour the cyder over them. Bake in the pre-heated oven for 40 minutes. Sprinkle with finely chopped fresh parsley before serving.

RECIPE

SUFFOLK PORK WITH APPLES AND CYDER SAUCE

Suffolk has long been famous for its pork, bacon and ham, and that tradition continues today – around 20% of the UK's outdoor-reared pork comes from the county, where the dry, sandy soil is ideal for outdoor pig-keeping. One of the largest independent pork producers in the country is Blythburgh Free Range Pork near Halesworth, where pork is produced from pigs living happy, natural outdoor lives, resulting in succulent meat with great flavour. See www. freerangepork.co.uk for more information. Use Suffolk cyder to make a delicious creamy sauce to accompany quality Suffolk-reared pork in this recipe.

 25g/1oz butter
 500g/1¼ lbs pork fillet or tenderloin, cut into small pieces
 12 baby onions or shallots, peeled and left whole
 2 teaspoonfuls grated lemon rind
 300ml/ ½ pint dry Suffolk cyder
 150ml/ ¼ pint stock
 2 crisp eating apples, cored and sliced but not peeled
 3 tablespoonfuls chopped fresh parsley
 100ml/3½ fl oz whipping cream
 Salt and pepper

Heat the butter in a large sauté or frying pan, and brown the pork in batches. Transfer the pork to a bowl. Add the onions to the pan and cook gently until they are soft. Stir in the lemon rind, cyder and stock, increase heat and boil for a few minutes. Return the pork to the pan, reduce heat and cook gently for 25-30 minutes, until the meat is tender. Add the apples to the pan and cook for a further 5 minutes. Use a slotted spoon to transfer the pork, apples and onions to a warmed serving dish, and keep warm. Stir the cream and parsley into the cooking pan, and allow the sauce to bubble so that it thickens slightly. Season to taste, then pour over the pork and serve whilst it is hot.

SUFFOLK SWEET-CURED HAM

A famous delicacy from Suffolk, although one that is becoming harder to find nowadays, is Suffolk sweet-cured ham. This was a widespread local way of curing ham in the past, when many country households kept a pig, and produces ham with a wonderful flavour. The whole process can take up to 10 weeks to complete, part of which includes steeping the ham for up to 6 weeks in a sweet pickling solution made of sugar, black treacle or honey, plus salt and saltpetre, during which the ham has to be turned every day. The ham is then hot-smoked over a fire of applewood or oak sawdust, a process that develops its characteristic shiny black skin, hence its other name of Black Ham. Suffolk sweet-cured hams are available from Emmett's of Peasenhall, as well as a range of other quality ham and bacon products. Emmett's also sell their products online – see their website www.emmettsham.co.uk

RECIPE

STEAK AND OYSTER HOTPOT

The photograph on the opposite page shows an early 20th-century view of the Butt and Oyster Inn at Pin Mill, a small hamlet on the estuary of the River Orwell south of Ipswich. The name of the pub (still in business) commemorates the oyster fisheries that used to be important on the river here. Nowadays excellent oysters are available a few miles up the Suffolk coast at Orford, south of Aldeburgh, from Butley Orford Oysterage, farmed from oyster beds in Butley Creek – see www.butleyorfordoysterage.co.uk. Oysters used to be plentiful and cheap in the past. They were often combined with steak in dishes like pies and savoury puddings to make the meat go further. Although oysters might now be seen as a luxury food, they add a wonderful flavour to this hotpot.

> 450g/1 lb braising steak
> 50g/2oz lard
> 2 lamb's kidneys
> 12 shelled oysters
> 1 onion, peeled and sliced
> 25g/1oz flour
> 600ml/1 pint water
> 675g/1½ lbs potatoes, peeled and sliced
> Salt and pepper

Pre-heat the oven to 180°C/350°C/Gas Mark 4. Cut the steak into small cubes about 1cm (½ inch) square. Melt the lard in a large pan, and brown the pieces of meat a few pieces at a time. Transfer the browned meat to a casserole dish. Skin and slice the kidneys and add to the meat in the dish. Add the oysters, reserving any liquor to use in the sauce. Cover the meat and oysters in the dish with the sliced potatoes.

Gently fry the sliced onion in the remaining fat in the pan until it is transparent. Sprinkle the flour over the onion, stir in and cook gently for a few minutes. Gradually add in the water and oyster liquor, stirring all the time. Bring to the boil until the sauce thickens, stirring all the time. When the sauce has thickened, season to taste and pour it over the meat in the casserole. Cover the casserole with its lid and cook in the pre-heated oven for 1½ hours. Then remove the lid and continue to cook for a further 30 minutes, so that the potatoes brown and crisp.

**PIN MILL, THE BUTT AND OYSTER INN
1909** 62001

RECIPE

SUFFOLK STEW

Suffolk's rich pastures provide quality beef and lamb. Begin preparations a day in advance for this hearty, satisfying stew. Serves 3-4, allowing 2 cutlets per person.

> 6-8 lamb cutlets, or one best end of lamb
>   (about 900g/2 lbs in weight), divided into 6-8 cutlets.
> 50g/2oz lentils
> 25g/1oz haricot beans
> 25g/1oz pearl barley
> 2 large potatoes
> 1 large turnip
> 4 carrots
> 4 onions
> 2 bay leaves
> ½ level teaspoonful salt
> ½ level teaspoonful black pepper
> 1 clove garlic
> 1 level teaspoonful mixed herbs

Soak the lentils, haricot beans and pearl barley in cold water overnight. The following day, peel and roughly chop all the vegetables; put them in a large saucepan. Trim any excess skin and fat from the lamb cutlets. Add these, together with the bay leaves, salt, pepper, crushed garlic and herbs to the vegetables.

Drain the lentils, haricot beans and pearl barley, before adding them to the pan. Pour over 1.8 litres (3 pints) of water, cover the pan with a lid and bring to the boil. Simmer gently for 3 hours. When ready to eat, spoon the stew into a warm serving dish.

**FRAMLINGHAM, VEHICLES ON MARKET HILL
1929** 82062x

AGENT
FOR
PULLARS
DYE WORKS
PERTH

LEISTON, SIZEWELL ROAD 1922 72579

RECIPE

TOAD IN THE HOLE WITH NEWMARKET SAUSAGES

Newmarket has a local delicacy, the Newmarket Sausage, but two companies in the town make it and there is much rivalry over which is the true version; however, both are excellent. Although there are several different flavours, the sausages made by Musks are made by mixing the meat filling with fresh bread, whilst Powters use the more traditional rusk; both companies use a closely-guarded secret spice mix in their products. Use whichever sausage claims your family loyalty to make this dish!

> 450g/1 lb Newmarket sausages
> 175g/6oz plain flour
> A pinch of salt
> 2 eggs
> 600ml/1 pint milk and water mixed
> 15g/ ½ oz lard or dripping

Make the batter 1 hour before you start cooking the dish. Put the flour in a bowl with the salt, make a well in the centre and break in the eggs. Beat them into the flour, gradually adding the milk and water to make a smooth, creamy batter. Beat it well, then leave to stand for 1 hour. (This can also be prepared in a liquidizer.)

Pre-heat the oven to 220°C/425°F/Gas Mark 7. Melt the lard or dripping in a frying pan and brown the sausages nicely all over (this gives a better flavour than cooking the sausages in the oven). Pour the fat and sausages into a 30cms (12 inch) roasting tin. Place the tin in the oven for a few minutes to heat through, then remove from the oven, pour in the prepared batter and replace the tin in the oven. When the batter is nicely puffed up, reduce the oven temperature to 190°C/375°F/Gas Mark 5, and continue cooking until well-risen and golden brown – the total cooking time from start to finish should be 35-40 minutes.

NEWMARKET, HIGH STREET 1929 81956

Flavours of ...
SUFFOLK
MEAT AND GAME

RECIPE

RABBIT CASSEROLE WITH DUMPLINGS

Rabbits over-ran much of Suffolk in the past, and formed a staple part of many country people's diet. This serves up rabbit portions casseroled with ale or beer – preferably made by one of Suffolk's famous breweries, such as Greene King at Bury St Edmunds, or Adnams at Southwold.

1 rabbit, jointed, or 4-6 rabbit
   portions, depending on size
25g/1oz lard or butter
25g/1oz plain flour
300ml/ ½ pint ale or beer
1 onion
1 carrot
1 large cooking apple
50g/2oz button mushrooms
A sprig each of fresh parsley
   and thyme
1 bay leaf
Salt and pepper

For the dumplings:
115g/4oz self raising flour
50g/2oz shredded suet
A pinch of salt and pepper
A little water, to mix

Pre-heat the oven to 180°C/350°F/Gas Mark 4. Melt the lard or butter in a large heavy pan, add the rabbit joints and brown them. Remove the rabbit from the pan and place in a casserole dish. Stir the flour into the fat in the pan, cook for a few minutes, then add the ale or beer a little at a time, stirring continuously until the sauce thickens. Pour the sauce over the rabbit joints in the casserole. Peel and slice the onion, carrot and apple, and add to the casserole. Chop the mushrooms and herbs, add to the casserole with the bay leaf and season with salt and pepper. Cover the dish with its lid and cook in the oven for 1½ hours before adding the dumplings. To make the dumplings, mix the flour, salt and pepper and suet with enough water to form a firm dough. Flour your hands and shape the dough into 8-12 small balls, depending on how big you want them. Place them on top of the casserole and cook for a further 30 minutes. Remove the bay leaf before serving.

Southwold suffered a fire in 1659 which destroyed most of the town, but its medieval church of St Edmund survived. Inside the church is 'Southwold Jack', also known as 'Jack the Smiter' and 'Jack Smite the Clock', a rather menacing brightly-painted wooden figure of a 15th-century warrior. His duty is to strike the clock with his battle-axe upon the pulling of a cord, thus announcing the beginning of services. He will be familiar to drinkers of Adnams beer, brewed in Southwold, as he features on the labels of Adnams bottled beer. There is also a similar figure, known as 'Jack-o'-the-Clock', in Holy Trinity Church at Blythburgh.

SOUTHWOLD, JACK SMITE THE CLOCK c1900 S168302

SOUTHWOLD, TRAFFIC IN THE MARKET PLACE 1906 56845y

SUDBURY, THE MARKET 1904   51156

SUFFOLK CHEESE AND BUTTER

Dairy production was more important in Suffolk in past centuries than it is today, but even so, no famous cheeses historically come from this area. Writing in the early 18th century, Daniel Defoe remarked that Suffolk was famous for 'the best butter and perhaps the worst cheese in England'. Suffolk Cheese was made from skimmed milk, using the milk left after the cream had been skimmed off for sale, or for making butter. It was generally sold to the poor in London. It was a very hard cheese and not at all popular, as evidenced by the famous diarist Samuel Pepys in the 17th century, who recorded how his servants complained about being given it to eat:

> *'And so home, where I found my wife vexed at her people for grumbling to eat Suffolk Cheese which I am also vexed at, and so to bed.'*
> Samuel Pepys, from his 'Diary' – 4th October 1661.

The excellent butter that Daniel Defoe referred to was made from the milk of the Suffolk Dun cow, an historic dairy breed that was noted for its high milk yield. The Suffolk Dun breed is now extinct, but is recalled in the name of several pubs in Suffolk called 'The Dun Cow'.

One of the places where Suffolk butter would have been sold from was the Butter Cross in the market place at Bungay, seen in the photograph on the opposite page. Bungay suffered a major town fire in 1688, and the Butter Cross was built to commemorate the disaster, and to provide the local farmers' wives with a sheltered place where they could display their butter and other produce for sale. It is a pretty octagonal building, with a dome surmounted by a figure of justice. In the past, a cage underneath the Butter Cross was used to hold felons to public ridicule, although by the time this photograph was taken, it was no longer in service!

**BUNGAY
THE MARKET PLACE
AND BUTTER CROSS
c1900** B617301

31

RECIPE

ELIZA ACTON'S WAY WITH BRUSSELS SPROUTS

The name of Mrs Beeton is familiar to many as the cookery guru of the Victorian period, but another very influential cookery writer of the 19th century was Eliza Acton, who lived in Suffolk for much of her life. Born in 1799 in Battle, Sussex, her family moved to live in a house in Dock Street in Ipswich soon after her birth, where her father was in the beer and wine trade. In 1845 Eliza Acton published her first cookery book, 'Modern Cookery for Private Families', which predated Mrs Beeton's 'Book of Household Management' of 1861 by several years, and proved so popular that it remained in print for over 50 years. Eliza Acton was the first cookery writer to use the now-widespread practice of listing the ingredients for a recipe, and also suggesting the cooking times. She also included the earliest recorded English recipe for Brussels sprouts in her book – here it is:

'These delicate little sprouts, or miniature cabbages, which at their fullest growth scarcely exceed a large walnut in size, should be quite freshly gathered. Free them from all discoloured leaves, cut the stems even, and wash the sprouts thoroughly. Throw them into a pan of water properly salted, and boil them quickly from eight to ten minutes; drain them well, and serve them upon a rather thick round of toasted bread buttered on both sides. Send good melted butter to table with them. This is the Belgian mode of dressing this excellent vegetable, which is served in France with the sauce poured over it, or it is tossed in a stewpan with a spice of butter and some pepper and salt; a spoonful or two of veal gravy (and sometimes a little lemon-juice) is added when these are perfectly mixed. 9 to 10 minutes.'

RECIPE

BUTTERED ASPARAGUS

Like other parts of East Anglia, Suffolk is famous for its asparagus, which is in season from May to early July. Asparagus should be cooked and eaten as soon as possible after being picked, preferably on the same day, for its flavour to be enjoyed at its best. To prepare the fresh asparagus spears, trim off any woody ends and lightly scrape off any scales from the lowest parts of the stems, scraping away from the delicate tips.

> 450g/1 lb asparagus spears, trimmed and scraped as above
> 25g/1oz butter
> 1 teaspoonful caster sugar
> Salt and pepper

Cook the prepared asparagus spears in a pan of lightly salted water for about 5-6 minutes, then drain well. Melt the butter and fry the asparagus gently for a further 5 minutes. Sprinkle the sugar over the asparagus, season to taste with salt and pepper, and serve.

Marsh Samphire, or glasswort, is a wild plant rather like asparagus that grows on the salt marshes around the Suffolk coast. It is often called 'poor man's asparagus', and is gathered for sale commercially when in season. The green fleshy tips of samphire should be washed and trimmed of any coarse roots, then steamed or cooked in boiling water for 6-8 minutes, until tender but still with some 'bite' to it. Samphire can either be served hot, with melted butter, or cold in a salad, with a vinaigrette dressing. It also goes very well with fish, shellfish and lamb – especially lamb that has grazed on the salt marshes.

RECIPE

SUFFOLK RED CABBAGE

This dish has a delicious sharp-sweet flavour that goes extremely well with game, roast pork or sausages. It also reheats well.

> 1 red cabbage
> 50g/2oz butter
> 1 slice of ham, thickly cut – weighing about 115g/4oz
> 2 tablespoonfuls vinegar
> 1 tablespoonful sugar
> Salt and pepper

Pre-heat the oven to 160°C/325°F/Gas Mark 3.

Cut the red cabbage into quarters with a stainless steel knife; remove the cores, then slice fairly thin. Cut the ham into little sticks about 3cms (1 inch) long.

Melt the butter in an ovenproof casserole dish and add the ham pieces. Let the ham simmer gently in the butter without browning for five minutes, then stir in the sliced cabbage and turn it over in the butter until it is all coated and glistening. Cover the pan and allow the cabbage to sweat for 10 minutes. Stir in the vinegar and sugar, season with salt and pepper and cover the dish with its lid.

Put the dish in the oven and let the cabbage cook very gently for 2 hours, stirring occasionally to make sure it doesn't stick to the bottom of the dish.

RECIPE

SUFFOLK CARROT PIE

Suffolk is one of the main carrot-producing areas of the UK. This makes a tasty dish to be served hot, and also makes a good accompaniment to cold meats.

> 6 carrots, grated
> 6 potatoes, peeled and grated
> 2 eggs, separated
> Salt and pepper
> 2 tablespoonfuls of plain flour

Pre-heat the oven to 180°C/350°F/Gas Mark 4 and grease an ovenproof dish.

Beat the egg yolks in a bowl and season with salt and pepper. Gradually stir in the flour to make a smooth paste, and mix the grated carrots and potatoes into the mixture.

Beat the egg whites until they form stiff peaks, and carefully fold them into the mixture.

Turn it all into the greased dish, and bake in the pre-heated oven until the pie is golden brown.

FELIXSTOWE, CONSTABLE ROAD 1907 58976

RECIPE

FELIXSTOWE TART

This is like a large shortcake biscuit base, with the centre covered with jam and a meringue topping. It can also be filled with stewed apples instead of jam as an alternative. This needs to be baked in something wide and fairly flat with a slight rim, either an old-fashioned shallow enamel pie plate, or on an oven-proof dinner plate, about 25cms (10 inches) in diameter.

> 115g/4oz plain flour
> 115g/4oz cornflour
> 1 teaspoonful baking powder
> 175g/6oz caster sugar (half for the dough, half for the topping)
> 75g/3oz butter or margarine
> 2 eggs, separated
> 2 tablespoonfuls milk
> Plenty of raspberry jam – you may need a whole jar
> A little extra caster sugar to finish

FELIXSTOWE, CHILDREN'S RIDES 1907 58978

Pre-heat the oven to 180°C/350°F/Gas Mark 4. Grease a shallow pie plate or an ovenproof dinner plate about 25cms (10 inches) in diameter.

Sift the flour, cornflour and the baking powder into a large bowl, add 75g/3oz of the sugar and rub in the butter or margarine. Beat the egg yolks with the milk, and mix into the flour until you have a soft dough. Roll out the dough on a floured surface to just under the size of your baking dish or plate. Lay the dough on the dish (or press it evenly onto the dish, if the dough was too sticky to roll easily), leaving the edges slightly thicker all round. Prick all over the centre with a fork, and crimp around the edges with your thumb, to decorate. Bake in the pre-heated oven for about 20 minutes, until it is crisp and golden but not over-browning at the edges. Remove from the oven and leave to cool.

Reduce the oven temperature to 150°C/300°F/Gas Mark 2.

When the tart base has cooled, fill the hollow in the centre of the dough base evenly with jam, but do not spread it over the raised edge. Whisk the egg whites until they are stiff, then add half the remaining 75g/3oz caster sugar and continue whisking to make a meringue mixture that holds its shape and stands in soft peaks. Reserve one teaspoonful of the remaining sugar and gently fold in the rest, using a metal spoon. Swirl the meringue mixture over the jam so that it is all covered, but don't spread it over the exposed dough edges. Scatter the topping with the last teaspoonful of sugar. Bake in the oven at the reduced temperature until the meringue is set and lightly browned – about 25-30 minutes.

RECIPE

THAPE PIE

'Thape' is an old Suffolk word for a gooseberry. Whit Sunday at the end of May was traditionally celebrated in Suffolk with a gooseberry, or 'thape', pie, served with custard. This was traditionally the first gooseberry pie of the season. This is an old-fashioned fruit pie, made in a deep, oval, rimmed pie dish with only a pastry crust over the top. This retains all the fragrant juice of the fruit, leaving the top crust crisp and separate.

<u>For the filling:</u>
900g/ 2 lbs young green gooseberries
175g/6oz caster sugar

<u>For the pastry:</u>
175g/6oz plain flour
A pinch of salt
75g/3oz lard or pastry baking fat
25g/1oz butter
A little milk
A little caster sugar to finish

First, make up the pastry by sifting the flour and salt together and rubbing in the fats to the 'fine breadcrumbs' stage, then adding just enough cold water to mix to a dough that leaves the bowl clean. Knead the dough lightly until it is smooth and elastic, then wrap it in cling film and leave it to 'rest' in the fridge for 20 minutes.

Pre-heat the oven to 220°C/425°F/Gas Mark 7 and grease a 900ml (1½ pint) deep oval pie dish.

Top and tail the gooseberries, wash and drain them, then pile them into the pie dish and sprinkle the sugar in amongst them.

When the pastry has been 'rested', roll it out to an oval shape about 2cms (¾ inch) larger than the top of the pie dish. Cut a narrow strip from around the pastry, dampen the rim of the pie dish and fit the strip around it. Brush the strip with water, then fit the pastry lid over the pie, pressing the two pastry edges together well to seal them, then knock back and flute the edges. Cut two holes in the pastry lid to allow steam to escape.

Bake the pie in the pre-heated oven for 10 minutes, then lower the oven temperature to 190°C/375°F/Gas Mark 5 and bake for a further 30 minutes until the pastry is crisp and golden. Dredge with a little more caster sugar before serving.

BOXFORD, CHURCH STREET c1955 B620021

RECIPE

MRS KENT'S LEMON PIE

This is named after an Ipswich housewife of the 18th century, a Mrs Kent, whose recipe for a lemon pie was recorded in a notebook by her friend, neighbour and local recipe collector Elizabeth Hicks. It is equally good eaten either hot or cold.

> 175g/6oz sweet shortcrust pastry (made in the usual way with 175g/6oz plain flour and 75g/3oz fat, adding in one dessertspoonful of caster sugar)
> 1 tablespoonful grated lemon rind
> 3 tablespoonfuls lemon juice
> 115g/4oz caster sugar
> 50g/2oz unsalted butter
> 4 eggs, beaten

Grease a small pie or flan dish about 18-20cms (8 inches) in diameter. Roll out the pastry on a lightly floured surface and use it to line the dish.

Put the butter, sugar, lemon juice and lemon rind into a small saucepan and heat gently over a low heat without stirring until the butter has melted and the sugar has completely dissolved. Remove from the heat and leave to one side until it is completely cold. Pre-heat the oven to 200°C/400°F/Gas Mark 6, and place a baking tray in the oven to heat up.

Strain the beaten eggs through a sieve to remove any white threads, and mix them into the cold lemon, sugar and butter mixture. Pour the mixture gently into the pastry case. Stand the pie on the baking tray in the pre-heated oven (this helps the pastry base to cook through) and bake for 10 minutes, then reduce the oven temperature to 180°C/350°F/Gas Mark 4 and bake for a further 15-20 minutes, until the filling is set and the pastry is lightly golden.

RECIPE

IPSWICH ALMOND PUDDING

Here is another old recipe from Ipswich, also known as Ipswich Pudding. This recipe includes orange flower water or rose water, which may prove hard to find, but most branches of Waitrose sell it – look for it near the gelatine and food colourings and flavourings on supermarket shelves.

450ml/15fl oz milk
150ml/5fl oz double cream
50g/2oz fresh white breadcrumbs
75g/3oz caster sugar
175g/6oz ground almonds
1 teaspoonful orange flower or rose water (see above)
3 beaten eggs
25g/1oz butter

Pre-heat the oven to 180°C/350°F/Gas Mark 4.

Place the milk in a saucepan and heat until warmed. Place the breadcrumbs in a large mixing bowl, and pour the warm milk over them. Mix in the sugar, almonds and orange or rose water and leave to soak for 15 minutes. Add the beaten eggs to the breadcrumb mixture and mix well. Pour the mixture into a buttered pie dish.

Place the dish in a deep roasting tin filled with enough hot water to come half way up its side, and place in the pre-heated oven. Bake for about 30 minutes, until the filling is set. Serve hot with cream or custard.

Flavours of ...
SUFFOLK
PUDDINGS AND PIES

IPSWICH, THE BUTTERMARKET 1893 32204

GOOD

CHEAP

STATIONERY.

GOO

CHEA

STATION

RECIPE

GREENGAGE FLAN

The greengage, or green plum, is named after Sir William Gage, who lived in the 18th century at Hengrave Hall near Bury St Edmunds in Suffolk. At some time before 1724 he was sent some plum trees from France by his brother John who was a Catholic priest there. The trees had lost their labels in transit so no one knew what variety there were, so the gardener planted them in an orchard on the estate and called them 'Green Gages' after his employer, later shortened/corrupted to 'Greengage'. The delicious yellowy-green fruit that they produced soon became very popular, described by the garden writer Philip Miller in 1731 as 'one of the best plums in England'. Greengages have a delicious sweet flavour, and are in season in late August and early September. They were very popular in Victorian times, and are currently coming back into popularity again. This recipe encases greengages in an open flan with a buttery, almond filling. It is not a traditional Suffolk recipe, but greengages go particularly well with almonds, which seem to intensify their delicious flavour. If you can't get greengages, you can use another variety of plum instead.

> 225g/8oz sweet shortcrust pastry (made in the usual way with 225g/8oz plain flour, and 115g/4oz fat, and adding 1 rounded dessertspoonful caster sugar)
> 450g/1 lb ripe greengages, washed, halved and stoned
> 115g/4oz butter, softened to room temperature
> 115g/4oz caster sugar
> 2 eggs, beaten
> 115g/4oz ground almonds
> Half a teaspoonful almond essence
> 25g/1oz flaked almonds (about 2 tablespoonfuls)

Pre-heat the oven to 200°C/400°F/Gas Mark 6 and place a baking tray in the oven to heat up. Grease a flan dish 22-24cms (8-9 inches) in diameter. Roll out the pastry and use it to line the flan dish. Arrange the greengage halves, cut side up, in the pastry case.

Beat the butter and sugar together until light and fluffy. Gradually beat in the eggs, a little at a time, adding some of the ground almonds if necessary to prevent the mixture curdling, then mix in all the ground almonds and the almond essence. Cover the greengages with the almond mixture, spreading it gently to form an even surface. Sprinkle the flaked almonds all over. Place the flan dish on the baking tray in the preheated oven (this helps the pastry base to cook through properly) and bake for 10 minutes, then reduce the oven temperature to 160°C/325°F/Gas Mark 3 and bake for a further 25-30 minutes, until the filling is slightly risen and golden brown, and feels firm to the touch. This is good served either hot or cold.

BURY ST EDMUNDS, CORNHILL c1955 B258044

RECIPE

SUFFOLK APPLE CAKE

Suffolk was once an important apple growing region. A famous Suffolk apple variety is the St Edmund's Russet, also known as St Edmund's Pippin, which was first recorded in 1870, raised by a Mr Richard Harvey of Bury St Edmunds. Both the apple and the historic market town are named after St Edmund, the 9th-century Anglo-Saxon king of East Anglia who was murdered by Viking Danes for refusing to renounce his Christian faith, and later canonised. His shrine in the now-lost abbey at Bury St Edmunds made the town a centre of pilgrimage in the Middle Ages. St Edmund was the patron saint of England until he was replaced by the more warlike St George in the 14th century. A campaign in 2006 to have St Edmund reinstated as the patron saint of England was unsuccessful, but in 2007 Suffolk County Council adopted him as its patron saint, and flags are flown throughout the county on St Edmund's Day, 20th November.

        225g/8oz plain flour
        1½ teaspoonfuls baking powder
        A pinch of salt
        115g/4oz lard or margarine
        50g/2oz caster sugar
        225g/8oz dessert apples (weighed after being peeled
          and cored), either grated or finely chopped
        A little milk

Pre-heat the oven to 190°C/375°F/Gas Mark 5. Grease a baking sheet. Sift the flour, baking powder and salt into a mixing basin. Rub in the lard or margarine until the mixture resembles breadcrumbs, and stir in the sugar. Add the grated or chopped apples, then just enough milk to make a firm dough, and mix well. Flour your hands and form the dough into a round, flat cake about 20cms (8inches) in diameter and about 1.5cms (¾ inch) thick. Place on the greased baking sheet and bake in the pre-heated oven for about 45 minutes, until the cake is well-risen and golden. Eat the cake hot, cut into wedges, split open and spread with butter.

BURY ST EDMUNDS, THE ABBEY GATE c1900 B25850I

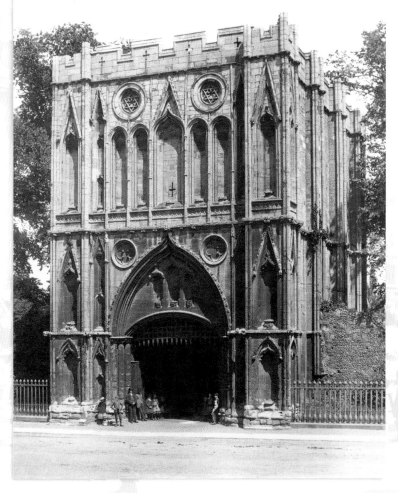

RECIPES

SUFFOLK FOURSES CAKE

This traditional lardy bread was served on Suffolk farms to harvest workers in the afternoons, together with a sweetened beer known as 'sugar beer'. It was probably named 'fourses' because it was served at the four o'clock break, although the name may also relate to the custom of marking the bread into four sections which was followed in some areas of Suffolk. It is a moist, light, semi-sweet cake that doesn't need to be spread with butter. It is also excellent served with cheese.

> 675g/1½ lbs strong plain flour
> 1 level teaspoonful salt
> 2 teaspoonfuls ground mixed spice
> 175g/6oz lard, softened
> 15g/ ½ oz dried yeast (3 heaped teaspoonfuls)
> 2 teaspoonfuls sugar
> 450ml/ ¾ pint warm water
> 175g/6oz currants
> A little milk to glaze

Mix the yeast with the sugar and a little of the warmed water, whisk it with a fork until it has dissolved, then leave in warm place for 10-15 minutes until it has activated and frothed up.

Sift the flour, salt and spice into a bowl. Rub in the lard and add the yeast mixture. Stir in the remaining water and mix to a smooth, pliable dough. Knead the dough thoroughly, then cover the bowl with a cloth and leave to rise in a warm place until the dough has doubled in size. Knock back, and knead in the currants. Either shape the dough into loaves and put into 450g/1 lb loaf tins, or shape it in to a large round and place on a greased baking sheet, and leave to rise again. If you are making the round loaf version, it is now traditional to mark the top of the loaf into four sections with a sharp knife. Brush the top with milk to glaze, and bake in a hot oven (200°C/400°F/Gas Mark 6) for 45 minutes, until well risen and golden brown.

SUFFOLK RUSKS

Traditionally, these crisp, lightly browned biscuits would have been made with yeast in a brick oven at the same time as the family's bread was baked, put in last, at the front of the oven, as they only take a short time to cook. They would then have been dried in the cooling oven after the baking was done, until they were brown and crisp. This modern recipe uses self-raising flour instead, which makes them very quick and easy to prepare. The stage when you take them out of the oven for the first time is important – they must have had time to rise and develop a slight split around their sides, but not be fully cooked. This amount should make 10-12 rusks.

> 225g/8oz self-raising flour
> A good pinch of salt
> 75g/3oz lard, butter or margarine (or 50g/2oz lard,
>   and 25g/1oz butter or margarine)
> 1 egg, beaten
> A little milk or water, if necessary

Pre-heat the oven to 220°C/425°F/Gas Mark 7, and grease a baking tray.

Sift the flour and salt into a bowl, and rub in the fat until the mixture resembles breadcrumbs. Mix in the beaten egg, adding a small amount of milk or water if necessary, to form a firm, smooth dough. Roll out the dough very gently on a lightly floured surface to about 2 cms (¾ inch) thick, and cut it into rounds about 7cms (2½ inches) in diameter. Place the rounds on the baking sheet and bake in the pre-heated oven for 10 minutes, until they are risen and golden, and a crack has developed around their middles. Remove from the oven and, when cool enough to handle, split each round in half with a sharp knife – carefully, as they will be quite fragile at this stage. (Or you can split them the traditional way, by pulling them apart with two forks.)

Reduce the oven temperature to 180°/350°/Gas Mark 4. Return the split rusks to the baking sheet, cut side up, put back in the oven and cook at the reduced temperature for a further 15 minutes or so, until they are dry and crisp, and coloured golden-brown. Cool on a wire rack.

These are delicious spread with butter, and perhaps jam, at breakfast or teatime, or served with cheese, or spread with bloater or kipper paste as a savoury snack. Store in an airtight container to keep the rusks crisp.

RECIPE

GOD'S KITCHEL CAKE

It was a particular Suffolk custom for children to visit their godparents at Christmas time and ask for their blessings. A small cake called a God's kitchel was specially made for visiting godchildren. There was an old saying: 'Ask me a blessing and I will give you a kitchel', and in Chaucer's 'Canterbury Tales', written in 1386, we find the lines: 'Give us a bushel, wheat, malt or rye, A God's kitchel, or a trip of cheese.'

> 450g/1 lb made-up flaky pastry
> 115g/4oz margarine
> 225g/8oz currants
> 25g/1oz sultanas
> 50g/2oz candied peel
> 75g/3oz sugar
> 50g/2oz ground almonds
> 1 teaspoonful powdered cinnamon
> 1 teaspoonful grated nutmeg

Melt the margarine in a large saucepan. Add the dried fruit, peel, sugar, ground almonds and spices. Mix well. Halve the pastry and roll one piece into a square about 30cms (12 inches) across – it should be rolled quite thin. Place it on a baking sheet. Moisten the edges of the rolled pastry with milk or water, and spread the filling on it, leaving an edge of about 1cm (half an inch). Cover with the second piece of pastry, rolled out to fit. Seal the edges well by pressing lightly together. Carefully mark the top of the cake with a knife into 6cms (2½ inches) squares, but without cutting through the pastry. Bake near the top of a pre-heated oven, 220°C/425°F/Gas Mark 7 until nicely golden brown.

Sprinkle with caster sugar and leave to cool for a few minutes, then divide into sections and leave them to cool on a wire rack.

SOUTHWOLD, 1919 69123x

FRANCIS FRITH

PIONEER VICTORIAN PHOTOGRAPHER

Francis Frith, founder of the world-famous photographic archive, was a complex and multi-talented man. A devout Quaker and a highly successful Victorian businessman, he was philosophical by nature and pioneering in outlook. By 1855 he had already established a wholesale grocery business in Liverpool, and sold it for the astonishing sum of £200,000, which is the equivalent today of over £15,000,000. Now in his thirties, and captivated by the new science of photography, Frith set out on a series of pioneering journeys up the Nile and to the Near East.

INTRIGUE AND EXPLORATION

He was the first photographer to venture beyond the sixth cataract of the Nile. Africa was still the mysterious 'Dark Continent', and Stanley and Livingstone's historic meeting was a decade into the future. The conditions for picture taking confound belief. He laboured for hours in his wicker dark-room in the sweltering heat of the desert, while the volatile chemicals fizzed dangerously in their trays. Back in London he exhibited his photographs and was 'rapturously cheered' by members of the Royal Society. His reputation as a photographer was made overnight.

VENTURE OF A LIFE-TIME

By the 1870s the railways had threaded their way across the country, and Bank Holidays and half-day Saturdays had been made obligatory by Act of Parliament. All of a sudden the working man and his family were able to enjoy days out, take holidays, and see a little more of the world.

With typical business acumen, Francis Frith foresaw that these new tourists would enjoy having souvenirs to commemorate their days out. For the next thirty years he travelled the country by train and by pony and trap, producing fine photographs of seaside resorts and beauty spots that were keenly bought by millions of Victorians. These prints were painstakingly pasted into family albums and pored over during the dark nights of winter, rekindling precious memories of summer excursions. Frith's studio was soon supplying retail shops all over the country, and by 1890 F Frith & Co had become the greatest specialist photographic publishing company in the world, with over 2,000 sales outlets, and pioneered the picture postcard.

FRANCIS FRITH'S LEGACY

Francis Frith had died in 1898 at his villa in Cannes, his great project still growing. By 1970 the archive he created contained over a third of a million pictures showing 7,000 British towns and villages.

Frith's legacy to us today is of immense significance and value, for the magnificent archive of evocative photographs he created provides a unique record of change in the cities, towns and villages throughout Britain over a century and more. Frith and his fellow studio photographers revisited locations many times down the years to update their views, compiling for us an enthralling and colourful pageant of British life and character.

We are fortunate that Frith was dedicated to recording the minutiae of everyday life. For it is this sheer wealth of visual data, the painstaking chronicle of changes in dress, transport, street layouts, buildings, housing and landscape that captivates us so much today, offering us a powerful link with the past and with the lives of our ancestors.

Computers have now made it possible for Frith's many thousands of images to be accessed almost instantly. The archive offers every one of us an opportunity to examine the places where we and our families have lived and worked down the years. Its images, depicting our shared past, are now bringing pleasure and enlightenment to millions around the world a century and more after his death.

For further information visit: www.francisfrith.com

INTERIOR DECORATION

Frith's photographs can be seen framed and as giant wall murals in thousands of pubs, restaurants, hotels, banks, retail stores and other public buildings throughout Britain. These provide interesting and attractive décor, generating strong local interest and acting as a powerful reminder of gentler days in our increasingly busy and frenetic world.

FRITH PRODUCTS

All Frith photographs are available as prints and posters in a variety of different sizes and styles. In the UK we also offer a range of other gift and stationery products illustrated with Frith photographs, although many of these are not available for delivery outside the UK – see our web site for more information on the products available for delivery in your country.

THE INTERNET

Over 100,000 photographs of Britain can be viewed and purchased on the Frith web site. The web site also includes memories and reminiscences contributed by our customers, who have personal knowledge of localities and of the people and properties depicted in Frith photographs. If you wish to learn more about a specific town or village you may find these reminiscences fascinating to browse. Why not add your own comments if you think they would be of interest to others? See **www.francisfrith.com**

PLEASE HELP US BRING FRITH'S PHOTOGRAPHS TO LIFE

Our authors do their best to recount the history of the places they write about. They give insights into how particular towns and villages developed, they describe the architecture of streets and buildings, and they discuss the lives of famous people who lived there. But however knowledgeable our authors are, the story they tell is necessarily incomplete.

Frith's photographs are so much more than plain historical documents. They are living proofs of the flow of human life down the generations. They show real people at real moments in history; and each of those people is the son or daughter of someone, the brother or sister, aunt or uncle, grandfather or grandmother of someone else. All of them lived, worked and played in the streets depicted in Frith's photographs.

We would be grateful if you would give us your insights into the places shown in our photographs: the streets and buildings, the shops, businesses and industries. Post your memories of life in those streets on the Frith website: what it was like growing up there, who ran the local shop and what shopping was like years ago; if your workplace is shown tell us about your working day and what the building is used for now. Read other visitors' memories and reconnect with your shared local history and heritage. With your help more and more Frith photographs can be brought to life, and vital memories preserved for posterity, and for the benefit of historians in the future.

Wherever possible, we will try to include some of your comments in future editions of our books. Moreover, if you spot errors in dates, titles or other facts, please let us know, because our archive records are not always completely accurate—they rely on 140 years of human endeavour and hand-compiled records. You can email us using the contact form on the website.

Thank you!

For further information, trade, or author enquiries
please contact us at the address below:

**The Francis Frith Collection, Oakley Business Park,
Wylye Road, Dinton, Wiltshire SP3 5EU England.**
Tel: +44 (0)1722 716 376 Fax: +44 (0)1722 716 881
e-mail: sales@francisfrith.co.uk **www.francisfrith.com**